Agnes McEvilly

# CHILD CENTERED
# EDUCATION

W0007609

AUSTIN MACAULEY PUBLISHERS™

LONDON • CAMBRIDGE • NEW YORK • SHARJAH

A CIP catalogue record for this title is available from the British Library.

ISBN 9781398473188 (Paperback)
ISBN 9781398473195 (ePub e-book)

www.austinmacauley.com

First Published 2023
Austin Macauley Publishers Ltd®
1 Canada Square
Canary Wharf
London
E14 5AA

Agnes McEvilly took the usual 'certificate in education' route to primary education, followed a few years later by a Bachelor of Education Degree. Ever eager to intersperse theory with practice, an MA in philosophy and education followed.

It was whilst pursuing the MA that she was introduced to the writings of Martin Heidegger, a twentieth-century German philosopher and educator; and Michael Oakeshott, a twentieth-century English educationist and philosopher. Both thinkers have had a profound influence on her conception of education.

Later, and after an induction into the mechanics of early years' education, she devoted the rest of her career to this sector.

I owe a debt of gratitude to many people for the realisation of this book. My deepest gratitude and admiration go to Dr Peter Jackson, who introduced me to Philosophy, in the first place. It was his endeavours to get students talking and thinking for themselves that led me to discover Michael Oakeshott and Martin Heidegger, educators who have left a profound impact. Thanks, Peter, wherever you are!

Many thanks must go to Elmire for her faith and confidence in my work, with the children and for urging me to write down my experiences, in the classroom.

Much appreciation, Ellie, for the creative flair and scientific knowledge you brought to the classroom. The children not only benefited hugely, but loved the experiments. Chats about education were always refreshing.

Much appreciation goes to Dominie for that wonderful 'Sheep-Farm Frieze' that adorned the classroom each summer term, afterwards, and for all those tips picked up in the process. Colleagues during a difficult time of change that challenged our own conceptions of education, talks of writing something, were never far from the conversation!

Thanks to my sister Lolly for facilitating the party in the aftermath of the Christmas celebrations at the pre-school, each year. It made for excitement among the children and more social time all around.

Thanks too to my sister Phil for her generous hospitality, as we repaired periodically to her welcoming home in Ballinagarde, especially those delicious Sunday dinners and apple tarts. No better interlude for the thought processes.

Last, but not least, I want to thank all those children whom I had the privilege to share so many learning experiences with over the years and from which we all benefited. Thank you for teaching me so much!

Acknowledgement is due to my sister Anne for articulating so clearly the logic of the approach adopted and for the confidence she inspired after reading the first draft.

Without the computer and technical expertise of Sebastian Kulig, a busy man in his own right, stress levels would be exacerbated. Thank you, Sebastian.

To revive energies, frequent cups of coffee are as much a reprieve as they are refreshing. Thanks to my ever-caring husband, Michael, and for a listening ear, as ideas and scripts were regularly regurgitated.

Acknowledgement must finally go to Austin Macauley Publishers, whom I have found to be encouraging, helpful and very professional throughout my engagement with them.

# Influential Educators 'Being and Time' by Martin Heidegger A Personal View

Contrary to Descartes' (1596-1650) belief that man is lord and master of the universe, naming what is, Martin Heidegger, in his famous book, *Being and Time*, having stripped language back to its original meanings, argued that this is not so. Human beings, he suggests, are not outsiders, by-standers, estranged from the goings on of the world, the truth limited to what can be deduced and known intellectually, to be the case!

Human beings, he believed, are part and parcel of, integrally related to and bound up with one another.

Man and world are indivisible. In knowledge and understanding, with a ring-side seat, as it were, rather than estranged on-lookers, with intimations of their own possibilities, the truth, Heidegger asserts, is more disclosure, than merely categorical facts; as much intuited, spiritually discerned, as categorically, deciphered.

Language thus takes on connotations of engagement, attunement, listening, openness and dialogue.

# Education Through the 'Lens' of Conversation

Michael Oakeshott likens education to a conversation, a 'conversation, between the generations', whereby the student is invited 'to look at himself, in the mirror of his inheritance', make what he will of it and thus make his debut on the world stage. In the process, he will acquire an identity, gainsaying the need for extraneous appendages, such as tattoos or body piercings, a post-modern take on Oakeshott's duffle coat or CND badge!

This chimes neatly with Heidegger's vision of the world, as a people, inherently connected and in relationship to one another. Conversation is as intrinsic to our existence, as engagement, listening, openness, attunement and dialogue are intrinsic to conversation.

What I particularly love about this metaphor for education – albeit, the classical version, is what Oakeshott had in mind – is that anyone can join the conversation, whatever the subject matter, at any time, early induction, a clear advantage. The student, no less than the scholar, can take part, browsing or feasting, contributing, or listening, for as long, or as short, whenever and wherever, the mood to learn provokes and leads and as otherwise determined.

# The Call and the Answer!

It was while teaching a reception class in a private school that I was asked to lead the team in the Nursery Department. "I want you to do there, in the Nursery, what you are doing here in the Reception class." Coupled to the throw away comment from a previous head teacher that, "You can get the best out of the worst of them," the positive response from children, generally and the supposition among some colleagues, that 'it's her soft Irish accent', that gave credence to the thought, that I must be doing something right.

After a brief induction into the mechanics of Early Years' Education, my adventures with the under-fives began! Subsequently repatriating to Ireland, I opened a pre-school.

# Introduction

It was when Enya was leaving, after a two-year stint, that her mother approached me with the injunction to 'write down what you do here' – on noticing my apprehension at the suggestion, that I commit my experiences at the pre-school to print – that brought home to me, the exigencies of fate!

Given that pang of duty and the expectations wrapped up in these comments, the aim of this book, is to shed a light on a practice, that is believed, did some children, some good.

While the stories related here tell of a particular Practice, analysis and conclusions are influenced by a wider experience.

# The Pre-School Classroom

From fixtures to fittings, displays to materials, the classroom mirrors the principles and values, suffusing the practice. Whether mending, or affixing, tidying, or labelling, the message is clear; here, there is a time for everything and where everything is in its place. The fundamentals in-situ, the only obstacle to learning, is learning itself. Welcome to Child-Centred Education.

# The Unspoken Aspirations of the Child

Mirroring the needs and unspoken aspirations of the child, the aim, in the words of Martin Heidegger, is to let learn. Translated, that simply means, to facilitate and do whatever it takes, in order that learning is unimpeded. It is not enough to provide the materials, no matter how up to date or attractive. Anything that distracts the child from meaningful and sustained engagement, be it excessive choice, undue noise or shifting ground rules, must be foreseen, mitigated, or avoided all together. Just as the foundation is constitutive of the sturdy house, so it is of the self-possessed child. And it is never too early to start. When the goal is the world and its treasures – the purpose of education – the how of getting there, will balk at nothing! The teacher personifies for the child, the secrets, education, has in store. Children will do, whatever it takes, to uncover those secrets.

# A Case in Point: Will I Stay
or Will I Go?

Standing in the middle of the room, on that first morning and beyond, Justin had that quizzical look, as he surveyed the scene, surreptitiously, from the corner of his eye. His twin sister, Jennifer, meanwhile, mingling, contentedly with her peers. There were no tears, nor was there any attempt to leave the room. Intermittent attempts, to engage him in the goings on all around him, were dismissed with a shake of the head! Anxious, as to how best to solve the conundrum, Justin, in due course, unwittingly, came to the rescue.

From the morning, he was observed making his way towards a small group of children, working diligently with Mobilo (construction material), he was hooked! From then on, he would leap at any and every opportunity to devour whatever presented itself, or, was presented, to him. At times, he would have to be reminded that we worked on a turn-taking basis! He proved to be a boy of exceptional ability, keenness and ambition, advancing, to excel in all fields.

The importance of relating this incident is, I suppose, to reinforce the fact that, inside every child, irrespective of age or apparent indifference is a personality waiting to express itself. Captured by the rhythm and flow of life inside this

15

purposeful environment, it appears Justin had found his loadstone!

# A Holistic Approach to
# Early Years' Education

Thus, conscious of the uniqueness of each child, native inquisitiveness and the need to belong, children are geared from the outset, towards life in all its fullness. Since we have no other choice, according to Michael Oakeshott, as we navigate our way in the world, but to learn, we must capitalise from the beginning when primal instincts and education intertwine.

Themes and learning pathways, thus aligned with the happenings and necessities of life, form the kernel of the curriculum. From the seasonal, to the cultural, the mundane to the celestial, children are drawn into the ebb and flow of daily concerns. Growing into a sense of place and identity, follow suit.

# Learning: One Step at a Time!

The examples that follow are but a snapshot of the range of activities on offer. Learning to hang up coats, tidy away lunch boxes and materials, in general, are no less important skills and therefore, all part of the learning process. Creatures of habit, children like order, becoming adept organizers in no time at all and quick to remind anyone who forgets!

In the 'clearing', space is opened up for the free flow of the imagination. As children learn how to manage themselves, they progress to the more imaginative, interactive and adventurous types of play.

# Where Expectations Lead, Competence Follows!

Thus, dovetailing the orderly is the orderly introduction to materials and activities, one at a time. Table-top exercises such as, puzzles, board games, threading and simple construction, set the scene, for that gradual progression to more interactive and complex combinations once children have learnt the rules of the game and to work more independently.

Mutual bonds of trust and co-operation liberate both teacher and child, as together, learning progresses. In the process, children acquire perseverance, concentration and that ability to centre, the steppingstone to autonomy.

Once an activity is mastered, the child becomes very protective and even hostile to 'outside' interference!

Here I am reminded of the times I was rebuffed, as an arm covered the puzzle, or game, in an attempt to prevent, any 'interference'! The will to succeed, is, I suppose, a very potent driver of personal endeavour.

When the corollary is the case, even children of such a tender age, are very good at finding ways to sidestep 'work' and evade getting involved! Then it is a question of invoking parental help.

# Let the Conversation Begin!

Once children had settled at the beginning of the new school year, each would be asked to bring a photo of themselves into the pre-school. These would be mounted in a prominent place in the classroom. Names would be added, the teacher scribing, while letters were named and sounded. A coating of glue, the child's first encounter with that all important enabler, gave way to a sprinkling of the famed glitter, its application, a skill in itself, as yet to be perfected. The stencil would come to the rescue to complete – once glued and glittered – this photo gallery. Numbers three and four, were on their way to the memory bank!

This cheerful display, the subject of much observation, discussion and analysis, was what set the ambience that this pre-school exuded. It was an ideal focus, round which children could get to get to know each other, bond and communicate.

New recruits to the pre-school would, on arrival, sometimes lay claim to a particular photo! 'That's me' was not an uncommon remark! This particular age group share characteristics that, as they grow older, disappear. But they too, would be invited to add their 'credentials' and take their place in this gallery of fame!

# From Simple Beginnings!

Play-Do is the perfect stuff for the child finding his feet as it is for the solitary, or those with a more gregarious disposition. Competing, as to who can mould the longest snake, or, the fattest worm, Play-Do, is the catchall material! When outside is off limits, it can be a Godsend and when the inspector calls, manna, from Heaven! It can be as much fun scrambling and unscrambling, as it is patiently delineating, specifics. The teacher can insert herself into the goings-on when the imagination needs rebooting, or when the time is ripe to raise expectations.

# Sand and Water Play

There is no better place to expand horizons, bond and develop the art of conversation, than round the sand or water-tray. Whether it is experiencing the sand, slipping through the fingers or 'waterfalls', cascading from bottles, worlds of exploration and fun, are opened up. From stones to shells, small world toys to discarded containers, the 'anatomy of life' unfolds. This is where the teacher can intervene, when appropriate and where concepts such as sinking and floating call for experimentation and conversation. From burying to exposing, hiding to finding, sand is a great way to introduce young children to positional language. While subliminally, children are experiencing the magic of science, mathematics and social solidarity; they are enhancing their vocabulary and having fun, all at the same time! Experiencing something of the hazards of sand and water, and the art of the possible indoors, further challenge, children's coping mechanisms.

# Painting

Painting, with those broad-brush strokes, is beloved by young children and one of the staples of the early years' classroom. The ease of application, the allure of colour and the freedom it affords, enables the child to experiment and express, what it perhaps, otherwise, cannot. In this sense, it is as much therapeutic, as it is an enjoyable, learning experience.

Knowing when to assist and when to steer clear, was a salutary lesson I learnt one morning, as I put the finishing touches, to what I assumed, was Patrick's dog! Bursting into tears, I realised he had no such intentions. Scrunching up the 'painting' and depositing it in the bin after apologising profusely, I handed him a fresh piece of paper. Back on track, he proceeded to satisfy the urgings of his own imagination!

# The Allure of the Translucent!

Water 'painting' was hugely popular, particularly in milder weather. Surrounding walls, flagstones, water tray, plant boxes and the lovely stone Dutch girl, standing a-top a circular fountain, or anything at all, could be subject to multiple coats! Thus occupied, sometimes for long periods, children were able to experience the freedom of the great outdoors, no less perhaps, than exercise a personal ambition! These instinctual choices answer a need beyond logic.

Opportunities for learning are all around us. All we have to do is open our eyes!

# The Autumn Frieze

With leaves aplenty, our first attempt at collective work was the Autumn Frieze. Together, a variety of the most attractive were collected and strewn onto the painting table, where pots of paint, in brown, orange, green, red and yellow, awaited. Then one at a time, the leaves were faced front down and painted all over, the adult, modelling to start with. Once painted, each leaf would be placed on a piece of A4 paper, painted side pressed down, using a piece of kitchen paper. Removing the leaf was an art in itself! This colourful display, names affixed, to which the children were drawn to naturally, would adorn the room, until Halloween eclipsed; autumnal splendours! Once completed, children had the opportunity to experiment by themselves for as long as it took.

For the rest of the year, children routinely picked up leaves at playtime, or brought them in from home, or picked them up on the way to school! One may wonder what is it about leaves that interest young children. Could it be that newfound skill of turning a leaf into a pretty picture? Or could it be the realisation that a leaf is not just something to trod on! Things become meaningful, once experienced, for oneself.

# Still Life

Still life, is possible, with gentle nudges here and there and it is quite extraordinary the precision some small children exhibit once challenged! Surprised at the time, I once observed a colleague reproduce a masterpiece over several sittings aided by her preschool protégés. Expectations, creativity and, no doubt, latent talent, are a potent force.

# Construction Materials

There is a great array of construction materials available, nowadays, all of which have multiple benefits for young children, not least, their colourful appeal and geometric properties.

Lego, with its infinite possibilities and Mobilo's wheels, make these two particularly irresistible as witnessed, in the case of our former 'recalcitrant'! Both, lend themselves to conversation and the attendant free flow of ideas. Should interest wain, adults can join in, stimulate ideas and challenge the unadventurous! When it comes to Lego, structures can be added to and completed over time. The wheeled vehicles, resulting from Mobilo play, give rise to endless enjoyment for the individual, no less than the group. Your very own toys, toboot!

'Construction' play is a perfect antidote to the greater cognitive demands of language, or mathematical acquisition and often compliments the former, either running along in tandem, or, available, immediately, afterwards.

# Puzzles

Puzzles are such a great source of learning, that further comment is warranted. From the very simple to the not so simple, the larger to the more complex – here I have in mind those that come in 3D – there is a puzzle for everyone.

Subject matter is key – the natural world and real-life events, are, in my experience, more sought after, than the culturally popular – thus enhancing and consolidating, developing understandings.

While simple shape, number, or letter puzzles, reinforce the basics, the more complex, build on the basics and challenge emerging competencies. While they are a favourite for some, with every achievement, interest grows.

# Art and Craft

In due course, art and craft activities, afford multiple opportunities for wide-ranging learning. From texture to colour, shape to size, few subjects are off limits. The school year is replete with opportunities to get involved in life all around them, as the following incidences attest. But first, let us take a closer look at junk.

# Junk Days!

Anything at all, especially the colourful, shiny, or unique, was collected and stored. All for the 'rainy-day', or special occasions, as indicated in these reflections. What were termed Junk Days, were rare, but when they did happen, the flurry of activity and the general buzz was indicative of captured minds and creative hands! Junk Days only happened when children had acquired sufficient skills and the ability to work independently.

Preparation was, key. Tables would be covered to offset the worst effects of glue, in particular. Different types and colours of card and paper, miscellaneous bits, such as ribbons, stickers, glitter, old catalogues, mark-making tools and scissors, would be scattered along the tables. Adults would be on hand to help and sort out any problems that might arise, but the children were entirely free to make whatever they liked!

There may be neither rhyme, nor, reason, to initial and 'finished' concoctions, and the uninitiated may gasp in shock, but children would be very proud to take these specimens home afterwards. Once parents were aware of the rationale, they played along heroically! Exercising newfound gluing or scissors skills outweighed logic for now! Later on, some children did turn out fanciful creations, often with a hint of realism.

In our post-modern times, pre-school 'art', can sit well alongside exhibits in our finest galleries! End results, aside, it is the space and time to hone developing skills and ideas, in a caring environment, that is important.

# The Creative Table!

The creative table, complete with the kinds of bits and bobs, pre-school children find irresistible – glitter and sparkling paper, in particular – would, from then on, be a frequent option. It is a great opportunity to reinforce cutting skills, perfect the art of gluing, while giving free reign to lively imaginations; conversation, all the while, in free flow! Taking home these creations can be the highlight of that day's work for some.

# Outdated, Maybe,
# but Useful, Yes!

Regarded as outdated in post-modern understandings of child-centred education, stencils, in my experience, have their place. With a stencil for every occasion, possibilities and options are as varied as individual states of readiness.

Anchored with a favourite – stencils come in all shapes, colours and sizes – for the child finding class routines challenging, or those looking for adventure, the stencil may be the novelty that leads to concentration, precision and the honing of vital fine motor skills, or the sharpening of developing interests. Producing your very own bus, animal, person, or whatever, can be very empowering for the child.

For those of us bereft of talent in the art department, they are a Godsend! The times I had to endure comments such as, 'that's not a very good cat' or 'that looks funny', are too numerous to mention!

# Rubbing Boards

We would not dream of taking pre-school children to a castle or ancient church for a brass-rubbing experience. The skill, however, is not beyond little hands. Small-ridged boards, in a variety of designs, provide an excellent opportunity for the more adventurous. It is not easy to manipulate rubbing-board, paper and pencil at the same time! No matter how imperfect, children learn patience, concentration, confidence and that feeling, I did it! Some are ever ready for a challenge providing it is not completely beyond them.

# Outdoors

The burgeoning outdoors of spring, summer and early autumn can find us out and about – weather permitting – admiring the new-born lambs, to picking wildflowers or blackberries. Adorning teachers, carers, or classrooms with Mother Nature's bounty is redolent of that sense of belonging when children feel at home in the world.

# The Saint Patrick's Day Parade

It was the St Patrick's Day Parade to which the children were invited each year, however, that brought home to me the benefits of cross-curriculum activities. Here the historical, cultural, social and artistic, are woven into our national saint's story. Whether catching up with the boy, Patrick, looking after sheep, in the far northeast of the country and sending us scurrying to the map – which, for whatever reason, never fails to enthral young children – to the very mention of snakes, everyone was captivated. Our snake 'dictionary' would be invoked for colours and types and personalised preferences would be carefully coloured and affixed round the 'map', making their way to the sea!

Walking down the high street of the local village, bedecked in our national colours, waving those flags that had been carefully painted and picking up the coveted trophy before posing for that photo – that would later be displayed at the Pre-School, to add to our collection – was, no doubt, the highlight for the children. The colour, sounds, buzz, flag-waving, sense of bonhomie, fun and cheer surrounding this event will stay long in the memory of these young citizens.

# Halloween

Halloween allows us to dabble with the spooky as the darker days of impending winter draw near. Festooned in spiders, bats, skeletons and the odd witch, all of the benign sort of course, the classroom provides a reassuring place for the imagination to entertain the darker side of life! Those who cared to morph into witches added to the fun. The candle on the lunch table, flickering in the spooky pumpkin, is a reminder that the light is never very far away. Once they feel safe, nothing thrills young children more than the frightening!

# Christmas

For about one month prior to the holidays, tinsel, glitter, ribbons and glue, became the order of the day. What with the good will that surrounds the nativity story and the impending visit from Santa, it is a pivotal moment for wide-ranging work on language and for bonding and sharing.

Old Christmas cards are the staple that morph into greeting cards, pictures and stockings while kitchen tubes form the kernel for angels, snowmen and crackers. Interspersed with such industry and sometimes, simultaneously, the interactive crib, is erected. To reinforce understanding, a Bethlehem scene, depicting that night long ago is undertaken, as books are trawled for the most appealing images. Decorating the Christmas tree only adds to the fervour as children wait their turn to hang their favourite trinket. At the same time, children are regaled as to the origins and history of the different decorations. With the twinkling of lights, Christmas is finally welcomed.

The highlight of Christmas and its memorable climax in the pre-school, each year, is what we termed the Christmas Celebrations! The nativity story would be re-enacted, the children having made the kings' crowns and wrapped their gifts. Weeks of practice, made for a rousing rendition of carol and song, accompanied by our very own percussionists, when the day finally arrived.

Family and friends could sit back as 'the Christmas Celebrations' revealed something of the goings-on prior to Christmas, at this particular pre-School. Acting out the nativity story brought enthusiasm and enjoyment, as only working together, can.

Savouring those self-made fairy cakes, iced and decorated that same morning, Santa's sudden arrival and the unwrapping of presents was, without doubt, the highlight for the children.

For the adults, it was the satisfaction that time and effort had paid off as with a minimum of hints and gestures, the children had brought the whole event to a conclusion that delighted their families.

At ease in company remarks as to how independently children could negotiate their way between 'acting' and socialising, without much adult angst, is the kind of reassurance that make it all so rewarding.

The benefits, subliminal, or otherwise, undoubtedly, make a major contribution to the sum total of individual and the collective wellbeing of these pre-school children.

# The Arctic

From the pictorial to the more informative, our lovely array of Arctic books took pride of place on the bookshelves, during the darker days of January. Memorialised in small Arctic animals, an Arctic scene was erected in a corner of the classroom inclusive of an igloo to which the children had easy access and to where many would repair, on arrival each morning. Story would follow the trail of the different animals as they strode over the ice and snow; the polar bear being a definite favourite. Art would take up where story left off resulting in our very own penguins. Morphing from small to medium or large sized plastic bottles, children would be commissioned to scour the literature for detail. Standing tall, he would emerge, yellow or white fronted, with a long black 'cloak', matching yellow beak and broad feet, enabling him to stand independently! It is humbling to witness the joy these simple but laboriously engineered penguins engendered.

# Ice

When we hit an icy patch of weather at the pre-school, the ice would be lifted from buckets, barrels, or other containers and thrown onto the grass for children to experience for themselves the properties of frozen water. Ice lollies were an after-play, summer treat, when the weather was very warm.

# When the Easter Bunny and the Spring Cross Paths!

As the weather improves, the days brighten and the spring flowers begin to adorn the pre-school surrounds, talk of the Easter bunny egg-hunt is only a matter of time! Thanks to Providence, we never had to resort inside, for this most exciting adventure! The many hedges, flowers, bushes, trees and willow-tunnel, made for ideal hideouts. Certain children soon realised that running around excitedly, but aimlessly, didn't bring the success their more thoughtful peers managed! There was nothing like the sight of those eggs being hovered up, to initiate more considered tactics! A bit of adult configuration in the end, ensured that the bunny was true to his promise and included everyone! At the same time, salutary lessons were learnt in a fun and engaging way.

# The Talents That Came Our Way!

Ever ready to take advantage of any opportunity that might benefit the children, special expertise was always very welcomed. And so it was when Dominie arrived for the summer. While ceramics was her speciality, fabric – fake or otherwise – was, no less amenable to her creative hands. Thus, the Sheep Farm materialised. While I would flounder, in search of a template, Dominie would reach for a shaggy piece from the fabrics strewn on the table and with the help of her tiny apprentice, eyes would transform this scrap of fake wool into its like, grazing in the field! Dogs would similarly emerge. The scattered cottages had multiplied as yet another addition was inserted! Little latticed fences demarcated the tiny fields where pretty flowers popped up here and there. The sun looked on from above. Trees completed this 'busy' farm which, from then on, took pride of place in the classroom during summer terms.

From inception to completion, it is impossible to quantify the learning involved in the course of this, or any other project.

Whether from observation, accident or direction, all knowledge is lodged in the memory bank, which over time will form unique tapestries of life. Nothing is ever lost or wasted!

# Science Experiments!

Having no expertise in this field at all, the arrival of Ellie, with an engineering background and a flair for the sciences, opened the door to novel ways of working with materials. Since experimenting is what comes natural to young children, it is not surprising that materials such as sand, paint, food colouring and different kinds of paper, inspired heightened expectation and generated huge excitement and commitment from the children. Waiting for experiments to 'morph' and take home the finished product, sealed these memorable occasions.

# The Work Bench!

Michael was a carpenter with a charming sense of humour to which the children, responded enthusiastically. He could also make things and he had interesting tools. This combination was too good to miss and so it was decided that he would create something that each child could own and take home eventually. And so the houses came about. Children learnt to file and sandpaper wood, tap nails into wood and apply glue. For that authentic look, little chimneys were added while skills were reinforced. Others could watch as each got a turn to play carpenter! The whole process gave rise to much chatter, excitement and speculation. These buildings could, no doubt, be whatever future need, demanded!

Another example of the valuable learning made possible, when need, interest and expertise, intersect.

# The Family Professional!
# The Nurse

The visiting nurse, dressed in her uniform, brought great excitement to the preschool as she modelled treatments on a doll all dressed up for the occasion!

Everyone got an opportunity to listen to heartbeats and have a 'wound' dressed in a plaster! Young children love plasters! They can be very dramatic around falls and injuries of any kind and so this was a great opportunity to allay fears and experience the healing power of the nurse and the 'magical' plaster! Everyone was delighted to take one home just in case!

# The Policeman

A visit from the policeman, in full uniform, was no less exciting. The highlight, for the children was, I suppose, figuring out how the handcuffs work, wielding the truncheon and trying on the helmet!

Such encounters grow children's social awareness, build trust and increase confidence. And as importantly, add to the armoury of play!

# Play and Young Children

Montessori tells us that when children lost interest in toys, she got rid of them. My own experience is that as children developed higher order thinking skills, simple toys were discarded or used as props. The creative sort, such as kitchens, farms, or any open-ended toy, could be manipulated to become anything! Junk can service a requirement as can the most expensive piece of apparatus! Young children demonstrate an amazing versatility when it comes to turning ideas into reality, to make life work for them. This seems a good place to link the child's curiosity, its play and its work and ask what is going on?

# 'But It Is Playtime'!

There are as many definitions of play as there are types. Essentially, play is an expression of the child's imagination to satisfy his need to learn and find meaning. For the young child, that can literally be anything which brings me to Tony.

Tony arrived in pre-school one morning eager to show me a little carriage from his train set. After due admiration, I suggested that we put it on a shelf as was our custom and make it available later at playtime. Shocked at my ignorance, he reminded me, "But it is playtime." In an effort to offset my discomfort, I hastened to reassure him, "But of course it is." Tony duly went to hang up his coat and put away his lunchbox in its assigned place and headed to his play!

Young children do not differentiate between making a puzzle on the one hand and rolling a carriage on the train track, on the other. The only differentiating factor for the teacher, I learnt that morning, must be the needs of the child.

# Pretend Play – The Shop

The shop was furnished with a cash register, telephone, paper and pencils, play money and a variety of household 'goods'. Real coins would be interspersed with the fake. From the familiar, to the exotic, samples with interesting shapes, were integral to the 'shop' collection, thus, packages, boxes, bottles and sundry items, were lined up for the taking! A variety of shopping bags and purses were on hand for purchases! To maximise the benefits, as I thought, a transaction would be demonstrated as change was laboriously counted out. What was interesting about subsequent play was that the children eschewed the queuing and calculations altogether – perhaps they had intimations of digital times to come – and instead, stuffed their shopping bags with 'goods' and their purses with the money! Walking away, purposefully, suggests that these children enjoyed the shopping experience, minus the drudgery of the calculative! Every moment is to be enjoyed!

# The Hair Salon

The hair salon was hugely popular. Fitted out with everything from washbasin to towels, shampoos to hair-driers, to combs, brushes and accessories, it was a frenzy of activity. A telephone and writing materials were available but employed more as parallel activities! Time-wasting add-ons were eliminated! Bookings and bills were for another time!

# Only for the Stoic!

Seated on a little chair, head thrown back, two or possibly, three 'hairdressers' might be washing, blow-drying and or combing all at the same time! Rough handling would not be too strong a word to describe the feverish procedures! It was advantageous for 'clients' to be of the stoic type! There could be slides piercing the scalp and bands and ribbons perched precariously on leave-taking. It was not unusual for the teacher, unwittingly, to so present herself as parents arrived at home time! It was great fun and where co-operation made it all possible.

With only one 'sitting' at a time, children acquiesced to the inevitable, making the most of a stint, or waiting patiently to slip in and have a go when the opportunity presented itself!

The salon never had to 'close', given its limitations, due to children's inability to share and take turns. Research shows that when children's needs are being satisfied, they can forego wants they otherwise would not. It was a wonderful exercise in 'making-do'.

# Dressing Up!

What strikes me about 'dressing up' for the most part, is that some children had no sooner donned their chosen outfit, but wanted it removed forthwith! Headgear, in particular, was more encumbrance than asset! The moral of the story is, I suppose, that at such a tender age anything that hampers free movement is 'taboo'. They did, however, enjoy what was known as, the beauty box! Here could be found all manner of hair accessories and jewellery, mostly discarded, or lost by children over time! Along with mirrors, hairbrushes, combs, hair bands, slides, bracelets, necklaces, watches and brooches, the beauty box played a prominent role in the 'salon', as it did in mums and dads play and that around dolls.

# Phantasy Knows No Bounds!

Further examples of imaginative play range from 'doctors' and the attraction of the stethoscope, in particular, to mums and dads, which usually evolved round home play. The 'open-plan' kitchen, allowing for several children at a time to get involved, made for convivial conversation and an abundance of opportunities to re-enact life in the kitchen. Tables would be laid out from the abundance of 'crockery' and 'food' available. (Real utensils, of the smaller or unusual shape, were features of our collection!) Anything that would appeal and arouse interest. Dolls could be enlisted sometimes and favoured food presented. Whipping, stirring, cutting and pouring were a common sight. Young children love the goings-on around mealtimes in particular. No doubt our cooking sessions left their mark!

# Story

Since anything can be play to a small child, story is no exception. It may come as a surprise to some, but for me, it stands out as one of the best ways to garner and sustain attention. When the pitch and storyline are aligned story has few competitors when it comes to igniting interest. Perhaps it is that latent desire for knowledge that is awakened? Maybe it is that lively imagination that is animated? Perhaps it is that native desire to be at the heart of things? Academics aside, what is important here is the satisfaction and sense of well-being generated.

Story is a great opportunity to exercise the rudiments of philosophy. Likewise, hypothesising as to what might, might not, or should be the case in a given context is great fun while simultaneously teaching children flexibility and open mindedness, all essential for good conversation.

It can also be an opportunity to check as to where particular children are in terms of interest, application and cognitive development. Timing is of critical importance here and the expertise of the teacher crucial.

# Savouring the Fruits of Learning

In the wake of such 'adventures', what is intriguing afterwards, is the sight of children trying to outwit a rival and sometimes, more than one, in their eagerness to lay their hands on the 'must' have book! Adventuring into the ramifications of the language, as indicated above, is perhaps the trigger for such enthusiasm. Perhaps it's the earnestness of the narrator? Perhaps it's the story itself or the illustrations, or a mixture of both? Could it be the impetus to relive the captivating! We'll never know. Absorption and enjoyment of the experience and a developing interest in books, is all that matters.

# Language's Phonetic Application

From its animation of the entire educational enterprise to its configuration that assigns meaning, language's phonetic application is no less amenable to young children. The anti-clockwise swirl, for example, comes natural to young children and incorporating the letter C, as it does, is not as onerous to form as some might think. From C, the letters A, O, D, G and Q (lower case) are not light years away, can set the child on his way to writing his own name and whatever else his talent and readiness allow.

When a child masters his name, letter, or digit, he will write it wherever he can. Repetition is the hallmark of learning. 'Signatures' found in copy books left around for children's random mark making, letter, number practice, attest to this.

# 'I Must Finish My Work Because I'm Going to Big School'!

The response of a four-year-old, when asked to tidy up as the beautiful weather beckoned us outdoors, one morning in early summer. Aware of his displeasure, I suggested he could return to it when we came back inside. (Normally, formal work would end at this point and toys would be made available). On returning to the classroom, I found our 'writer', ensconced at the writing table, waiting for me, having walked past the toys, en route!

What was it, one may well ask, about the seemingly difficult task of letter formation that so captured this particular child? Could it be intimations of personal possibilities that lie deep in all of us, according to Martin Heidegger, that triggered this child's interest in self-discovery? This child certainly had a mind of his own. According to Jerome Brunner, education psychologist, anything can be taught to any child. It is all about the methods and the timing.

# Ahead of Himself

The child is always ahead of himself, as it were, always eager to transcend what he can actually do by himself and later on, when that initial sense of wonder has passed, mastering the written word or any other skill for that matter, may become more chore than wonder.

White boards-cum-marker pens make ideal working tools for the pre-school child. Phonic games and associated materials are specifically designed to further enhance young children's linguistic prowess. For letter formation, the Jolly Phonics Series has few rivals. With its dot-to-dot letter-formation approach and its delightful pictures, crying out to be coloured, it proves popular every time.

While young children come to enjoy these activities alone, or in small groups, once animated by a teacher, left to their own devices, they lose their allure. The inert fails to animate. This chimes with what Vygotsky called the Zone of Proximal Development, that is what a child is capable of achieving with the help of a more knowledgeable adult and what the child can do by himself.

# Alphabet Sounds

'Zany zebras zoom through Zanzibar' is one of the more remarkable tongue twisters in the multifarious jingles that was 'Alphabet Sounds'. 'Two tired tigers take a taxi to town', is a close second! And the children loved it. There is no better way to develop listening and observational skills, than being poised to place the button on the appropriate picture, while attuned to the next sound and affording a playmate equal access at the same time. Children very often shared cards! During any one session, the cards may be exchanged two or three times. Such was the attractive nature of this 'game' that attention spans accelerated. For letter-phonic recognition and reinforcement this game is unmatched.

# You Are Your Name

The scope for wide ranging learning of this nature is legion. It was customary, at the start of each academic year, to laminate the children's names in bold letters on card of pastel colours. These name-cards became very popular as they got passed around until children familiarised themselves with the sound of that initial letter, and the more advanced, everybody else's, in no time at all! With the introduction of Gaeilge (the Irish Language) into the mix and sometimes a bit of French, the challenges were heightened and the enthusiasm, no less, infectious.

Concentration on end letters was only a matter of time. Transference to words that resonated followed suit. Children were well on their way to mastering the fundamentals of language, seamlessly and naturally. Versatility ensured that element of surprise and fun, for which children have a natural affinity.

# Learning Another Language

It is a recognised fact that the under sixes, enjoy a capacity to absorb information that will never be repeated. (Montessori). Learning a foreign language, such as Gaeilge (the Irish language) or, French, is no exception. Nor, according to the experts, does it lead to mental confusion. The mind, it appears, has an inbuilt 'filing system', whence learning is advantaged rather than impeded whatever the subject matter.

At the pre-school in question, children are introduced to simple vocabulary and idioms from the beginning. Drama and interactive activities are the methods employed. It may take some children a whole year before appearing to have imbibed a single word, but this is normal when learning another language. Observing more accomplished, or older children, having a go is a wonderful incentive. Utterance of the first word increases confidence and it is usually only a matter of time before words multiply. What is important, fluency or otherwise aside, is that their first forays into Gaeilge, (the Irish Language) will make its continuation in Junior Infants a lot less daunting.

# Fascination with French!

Having a fondness for the French language myself and on receipt of a book of nursery rhymes, complete with CD from a parent, who happened to be French, we decided we'd have a listen! In no time, everybody was hooked. That nursery rhyme book must have been the most coveted ever! We eventually learnt them by heart and several copies of the said CD were dispatched to parents on request. One particular parent informed me that consequent to her daughter 'falling in love' with the language, she would not now do Spanish later as had her sister! I am afraid Gaeilge took a back seat at that particular time!

# The Limits of My Language
# Are the Limits of My World

This incident, I suppose, underlines, as if that was necessary, that anything can indeed be taught to any child. Teaching is as much about the enthusiasm, expertise and ambitions of the teacher, for his pupils, as it is, about methods. Bilingual teachers, no doubt, enhance linguistic prowess. The more limited knowledge is, the more limited the horizons will be. Wittgenstein told us as much, when he said, the limits of my language, are the limits of my world, notwithstanding that spiritual dimension, Martin Heidegger, drew our attention to!

Education, in the liberal sense, wants to go beyond such limitation. To partake in conversations to come, it is never too early to begin. Foregoing immediate wants is the harbinger of more expansive and satisfying horizons and there is no time like, the present! Limitations are intrinsic to the human condition.

There are also useful board games and puzzles that can advance language development for young children. Everyday vocabulary can be readily absorbed too, by frequent dialogue and simple instructions.

# Mathematics

Whether learning to count, add, or subtract, there are innumerable puzzles, board games and other imaginative ways to induct young children, into the rudiments of mathematics. The dice, large as possible, can liven proceedings when the outcome is unknown! It is a challenge in itself, to roll a dice across the table; to forecast the number, a bit of fun! Individual small white boards present one of the easiest and most attractive routes to number formation. As a class, or small group activity, the larger version is unparalleled. It is then that reinforcement, comes into its own and when ideas can be extended. There are also an array of attractively laid-out workbooks, designed to familiarise young children with the basics, while, at the same time, developing fine motor skills.

Shape is everywhere! When done with the inside, there is the outside! Besides playing with shapes, as a discreet activity, children also enjoy using them as templates and the more adventurous, arranging them into houses, trains, robots, or people.

# Tap-A-Shape!

With its corkboards, miniature hammers, tiny nails, colourful shapes and durability, Tap-A-Shape had it all. Whether alone or collectively – which could include the teacher – Tap-A-Shape, notwithstanding the immersion in shape itself in all its guises, lent itself to whatever inspiration dictated. The creative, no less than the child struggling to manipulate the different moving pieces, could participate and benefit. In time, some children would forego the shapes altogether and hammer the nails directly into the cork! This was not encouraged as it was not easy to extricate them!

It can be assumed, nevertheless, that these particular children derived some benefit from so doing? Montessori once said that if a child is concentrating, do not disturb them because they are learning something! Concentration, perseverance and precision are key components of learning.

Catering for six children, at any one time, Tap-A-Shape could prove a blessing, especially during pressure points such as unannounced inspections, impending social, or weather events!

For volume and capacity, we need look no further than the baking table, sand, or water trays. Organized games, in particular, lend themselves to estimation, counting and positional language. Frequent counting of children and equipment is par for the course, whatever the education setting.

# Making the Best of
# a Situation!

The tarmacadam playground is not only where children ride bikes and tractors, it is here too that we head, when wind or wet surfaces allow only the briefest of sojourns, outside. It is then that the number ladder and well spaced-out shapes, come into their own. To offset falls and collisions, finding the correct shape, makes for more considered manoeuvrings! Finding and lining up on a particular number, forestalls the rush to be first and alerts the thought processes! What the number ladder and shapes do for mathematics, the caterpillar does for Language! With the intermingling of the spontaneous and the fortuitous, mathematics and play become indistinguishable. Outside of weather events, they could be negotiated, at will.

Sometimes, while parents dallied chatting, these number and letter games claimed attentions that otherwise might preclude such social encounters. Mathematics, as we witness here, is woven into the warp and weft of pre-school life.

# The Variegated Nature of Learning!

Techniques such as these can be applied across the curriculum as testified by the author. The important thing, in all of this, is not the 'accumulation' of knowledge, for its own sake, but the imbibing of those 'scholarly' skills that not only feed the epistemic instinct (Abbs, 1994) facilitate the orderly mastering of the basics, but equally important be transposed across the curriculum.

This is not to suggest that the only 'end' of education is academic. Application, precision and industry are life skills, transposable to the home, games field, or wherever the imagination leads. Research shows, despite popular opinion, that those who excel in the classroom, are invariably, captains in the games field! My own experience is that the child who is master of himself, thrives on all fronts!

# Drama and Its Wide-Ranging Scope

Music and drama are great ways to engage young children and also great fun. Not only do they provide opportunities for showing off all those songs and rhymes, committed to memory, but for individual children, or small groups, to entertain family and friends. The whole class can be involved in dramatizing stories, such as the Nativity, the Enormous Turnip, The Three Little Pigs or The Three Billy Goats Gruff, for example.

# The Power of the Possible!

There is no limit to possibilities other than teachers' personal preferences. Drama can be hugely popular with the under-fives. Whether it is the freedom it affords, the challenges it poses or the chance to demonstrate 'talent', or that opportunity for self-expression, is impossible to know. One thing we do know is that it is good for language development, confidence building and bonding. When children are enjoying themselves, they are more amenable to listening, following instructions and waiting their turn, all essential building blocks of learning.

Another interesting fact is that sometimes very shy, diffident children, come fully into their own, often to the surprise of everyone. Sometimes, children, reluctant to get involved, will suddenly change their minds! Again, we can never be sure why this is the case. Initial dislike for a particular genre may be reversed once others are seen to be enjoying themselves? Perhaps, it is the realisation that it is not that daunting after all! Perhaps it is the impetus to be as good as their more confident peers? Perhaps it is that first chance to excel? What is important, in terms of development and well-being, is the enjoyment, challenge and sense of fulfilment experienced.

# Music

Music too, with its rhymes and rhythms, its soothing harmonies and gratifying tones, is beloved by young children. Reaching places, nothing else can, music releases energy, provokes movement, positivity and builds confidence. Music can be a happy release for the more solitary child especially for anyone on the autistic spectrum. Action songs and dance can be great fun and welcomed, especially in inclement weather. For those with latent talent, music must come as a blessed relief from the sometimes-discordant sounds of pre-school prattle.

To enhance independent learning, the pre-school classroom is furnished with percussion instruments, rhymes, songbooks, tapes and CDs. As music chimes with inner sensitivities, bursting into song comes naturally to young children, as yet, untroubled by self-consciousness.

We were accustomed to making our own shakers; fillings, a choice between rice, sand, or a mixture of both. Adornment was usually self-adhesive sign material, which came in lovely primary colours, (garnered for free), itself, a challenge in expertise and patience! The children were very proud of their very own instruments! Some added theirs to the 'music' box, while others took them home.

# When It All Comes Tumbling Out!

Hurrying through her lunch each day before scurrying to the carpeted area, songbook in hand, Peggy, would burst into her favourite tunes! Whether it was to entertain the rest of us, 'show-off', while the parents waited to take someone home, or just satisfy some personal need, I have no idea. I'm reminded of another, routinely, commandeering the French songbook. There is no knowing the whys of these instinctive preferences; all that matters is that these children were relishing the rhythms of sound and new-found confidence, while satisfying a personal need. If they saw themselves as in-house entertainers, maybe time will tell!

# Possibilities!

And yes, we're talking about pre-school children! Oh the possibilities and we mustn't squander them! Music also helps young children centre, become more attuned to the nuances of sound in its wider application, thus reaping benefits across the curriculum.

# Cooking: The Magic of Science!

Cooking is not only enjoyable for young children – all that rubbing in, whisking, stirring, beating, kneading, rolling and peeling – it is truly interdisciplinary, addressing a wide range of curriculum and developmental ends. There are few better ways to cultivate observational and disciplinary skills, than being poised when your turn comes to beat eggs, rub in butter, knead dough, or do any of the multiple jobs preparing food for the table involves. Any distraction could mean that coveted opportunity missed! This is not to mention the sensorial delight of smells wafting through the air as the patiently 'engineered' concoction emerges from the oven!

The sensorial, linguistic, scientific, mathematical, social and health benefits of the culinary in the early years' classroom exemplify the subliminal benefits of organized activities.

# Fairy Cakes

Clearly visible and opened at the correct page, ingredients and required tools, clearly laid out, the recipe book signalled fairy cakes, the perfect example of the multidisciplinary benefits of baking in the early years' classroom. Sharing out the different ingredients makes for busy hands and lively chat. Since the wooden spoon replaces the hand, concerns over hygiene are minimised.

Creaming the sugar and the butter is hard work at first, but, after the adult has demonstrated, children are ready for the challenge! The eggs can be shared between bowls and at the same time, the icing can be prepared and the cases put in the trays and counted, while the flour is spooned into the frothy egg, keeping waiting times to a minimum. Stirring the egg into the creamed sugar and butter was eagerly anticipated. The end was in sight! Carefully filling the paper cases with the mixture is a delicate balancing act! Children would take turns with the washing up.

Once out of the oven, the fairy cakes would be brought to the classroom for that oven-fresh smell! Necks would be strained as oven gloves made clear danger lurked! Once cool, they would be iced; each child, in turn, spooning, levelling and topping off with a favourite treat!

Orchestrating the entire business calls for dedication, commitment and patience! Sometimes, parents would be in disbelief as to the possibility of baking with any number beyond one! But it is possible. We all love fresh fairy cakes, straight from the oven! Children are no different.

Whether it is the allure of the end product, the excitement of the whole experience, or a bit of both, we can't know for sure. We do know for sure, though, that at the very mention of cooking, eyes light up!

I have a hunch that following these baking days, pressure may have been applied at home to replicate these delights! It is only a hunch, nobody ever complained. Once the children were happy, the families were totally supportive of every endeavour.

# Pancake Day!

Shrove Tuesday, better known, in these post-modern times, as Pancake Day, was celebrated each year in the pre-school, with a trip to the kitchen to witness that toss in the pan! Similar in ingredients and processes to the fairy cake mix, it was squeezing the lemon, or spreading the jam or honey, for that yummy taste, that was, no doubt, the highlight!

Heralding, the start of Lent, luxury ingredients had to be used up, so the children would be told, so that people could turn their attention to spiritual matters. Whether one is a Christian or not, a bit of self-restraint never harmed anybody. We now know that a balanced life is the secret of health and happiness. In this vein, children would be encouraged to try harder, but leaving the abstinence to the adults!

# Physical Education

Physical education opens all kinds of doors to learning for the under-fives. From running around, which comes naturally, to 'scavenging' and its attendant earnestness; there are times when the intervention of an adult is called for. There are innumerable ring, ball and hoop 'games', configurations, limited only by the imagination, that can enthral young children. Throwing and catching is much enjoyed, as is racing each other! The teacher joining in, only adds to the fervour. Organized games are useful ways too to counter inclement weather conditions, when roaming and climbing lose their appeal.

# Playing Together

It is necessary too that young children learn to play together for it is then those essential skills, such as, listening, waiting, taking turns and learning to respect the rights of others, are nurtured. And, just as importantly, life skills, such as these, are transferable across the curriculum and beyond.

# Consolidation of Language Skills

Language is the glue that binds all these activities into meaningful contexts. There are few better ways to understand mathematical concepts such as spatial awareness, numeracy and positional language than organised games.

# The Natural World and Its Fascination for Young Children

Nature fascinates all of us, not least young children. Anything that moves; creatures too small, or of little interest to most adults can engage small children in rapt attention for long periods. Here, the future Attenboroughs can be detected! When this happens other children and even adults can be drawn into the undergrowth, which hitherto was just a way to something more interesting! Magnifying glasses and repositories for finds become the order of the day. 'Research' sometimes follows when encyclopaedias, dictionaries and other sources of information are scoured. Young children are on their way to scholarship!

# A Born Naturalist

If is outside that I, myself, feel most at home, it would not be creatures of the undergrowth that would be the attraction! For Martha, it was! Irrespective of the weather, she would spend her entire playtime in search of whatever moved! On those occasions, when no caterpillars could be found, nothing would satisfy her disappointment until others were enlisted in the search. Failing that, adults would have to dig deeper to allay frustration!

Due to Marta's affinity with nature, we all learnt to be more observant and less fearful of life under our feet!

# Venturing Beyond the Pre-School!

Walks down country lanes, picking blackberries or wildflowers, spotting animals in the fields as well as greeting friendly cats and dogs en route, are all very enjoyable pursuits for young children. While learning about the world around them, they are, unwittingly, learning road safety and the manners of life.

# The Miracle That Is Nature

We read in the New Testament that we reap what we sow. For the young child, it is the discovery that overnight; his carefully husbanded plant has germinated or noticing on his return to the pre-school, after the Easter break, that the willow tunnel has come alive! Watching faces light up at such 'magic' is the stuff of fairy tales.

# Gardening: From Flowers to Vegetables

Hyacinths would be potted each autumn to be taken home around Christmas time or early in the new year. This gave rise to a whole plethora of activity; from name labels and phonics to the decoration of pots, to testing soil if dry or needing water. It was what pre-occupied some children as they rushed in to check their developing plant on arrival at the pre-school each morning. And there is nothing like enthusiasm to evoke like-mindedness in others! It was an interesting way to reinforce name recognition for younger children, or those developing at a different pace. The excitement and chatter when colour began to appear in each particular plant was only outmatched when the day finally arrived to take them home and show them off to family and friends.

# Growth: Experimenting with Light and Water!

It is well known that experience is the best teacher. And so, cress, for example, which is very easy to grow indoors, would be placed in a cupboard, watered occasionally, but left in the dark, as opposed to another sample, left on the windowsill and similarly watered. Very quickly, an observant three-year-old could see that the one grown in the dark remained pale and sickly. This simple experiment taught very young children that plants need light and of course, water to flourish. We can leave photosynthesis out of it for now!

Growing plants in pre-school teaches children many valuable lessons. Apart from the expectations generated and the introduction to plant husbandry, children gain insight into the miracle of nature, in its timely and assured processes.

It was customary to replicate the hyacinth experience, with a summer equivalent and all designed to immerse children in the natural world widen horizons and delight the senses.

# The Humble Potato!

Blessed with plenty of outdoor space, gardening was second nature to children who crossed the threshold of this pre-school. Given that most children are familiar with, what for many, is still one of our staples, it is not too surprising that we would grow some. Children would gather round and, in turn, scoop the earth into the container. Once the potato seed was earthed, it would be watered, then labelled and dated. Dating was very important. Little eyes kept an eye on the slow to emerge stalks, watering, as needed. Finally that day arrived in June to savour the fruits of patient observation and care. We would wash them in the classroom, boil them and share them at lunchtime!

# Carrots!

Carrots, too, that beloved snack, of small children, would likewise be sown in the spring. The children would stand around patiently waiting their turn to shoot the seed through the dispenser, into the given hole, when it would be covered in by the adult. Again, the children kept an eye for any signs of life as they skirted round at their play. When sufficiently advanced, some would be pulled, washed and savoured.

# Fruit Bushes and Trees

Black and red currants, gooseberries, strawberries, plums and apple trees flanked the grassy playground. Sampling these delights were all part of the playground experience, if, and when fruit was available. As we know, the right weather at the right time is the secret of a good harvest! Children had to wait till September to sample the plums! But then, what is time to the under-fives!

We cannot quantify the long-term benefits of such immersion in the natural world, other than its sensorial delights. We can only hope that children will always find shelter in her welcoming embrace,

# The Willow Tunnel

Because the willow-tunnel straddled the centre of this playground and was the focus of its attraction, it is worthy of special mention. It is to the tunnel that the children would head once through the little silver gate leading to the playground. Some would wind their way through the oval arch, through its curves, emerging through the igloo, at the other end. Others would chase each other round the outside, shrieking at the sheer delight of being outside. As that initial excitement waned, children could be observed wheeling the wheelbarrows through, or sitting in little groups – especially if the weather was very warm – chatting.

# When the 'Wolf' Would Show Up!

There was nothing like a visit from the 'wolf' in the environs of the tunnel, (an adult with a fur coat, over his head) to arouse frenzied excitement and 'terror' at the same time! Perhaps its reputation from the literature has not done him any favours but has left us, wanting to know more! Whatever the reasoning, the children would scurry away, shrieking in 'terror' and in the same anxious breath, begging for more!

# The Den

When feeling more creative, or in need of more 'privacy', others would make 'dens', knitting skipping ropes or the next best thing and 'fencing off' a secluded spot! Children sometimes love to get away from adults and experiment. Perhaps they feel such adventures will be frowned upon? Or perhaps, they are for a 'select' few? Again, we'll never know. It is all part of the early years' experience. What such ingenuity tells us is that when young children want to do something, they will find a way!

# Prayer

The perfect antidote to life after play and the excitement that can usher in lunchtime, soothing tones, reflections on a morning's work, life's wonders and or a simple prayer, can set the scene for the communality of mealtime.

# The Circle, the 'Lynchpin' of the Pre-School Classroom

Circle Time, synonymous with the carpeted and soft-seated area of the classroom, is like the anchor that helps stabilise the situation when things become choppy. Children have their moments, as they say, so there is no better forum for reconnecting and bonding, than the circle. In the particular practice, under consideration here, most activities either began or ended in a circle. Whether it was setting the scene for some activity or other, reading a story or, recapping on work accomplished or needing further explication, the circle, is where you would find us. Likewise, when problems arose, or rules needed revitalising, the circle was where harmony was restored. The circle was also where children convened, unsolicited by adults, where ideas were hatched and where rest and comfort were sought after, when little minds and hearts had exhausted themselves, while, others perhaps, were in the process of regrouping! Since this area doubled up as the library, looking at, or sharing books, was routine.

# The Fire Drill!

Even the mandatory fire drill can be an occasion to learn. When a four-year-old alerted me to the mixed messaging of the man running in the fire-sign and my insistence that they walk, in response to the fire-bell, it was that duty of care that saved the day! No one must fall and be left behind! Satisfied, the child in question skipped off!

# Behaviour Unbecoming

Lest the impression has been given that life inside this particular setting was populated with only the ethereal sort, it must be said that, over time, we had our share of what we euphemistically refer to as challenging behaviours!

Routine checks and balances, exhortations to emulate their own, or others' best would always be invoked, before more punitive measures were considered. Rousseau's dictum of not yielding, or all will be lost would, all the while, assault the ears! While I like to think that it is never too late to change one's ways, as we know from experience, it is always better to nip things in the bud!

# Spirituality, That Which Suffuses Life Itself!

Spirituality is one of those nebulous concepts, impossible to define exactly. It can best be described as that capacity to capture the awesomeness of life: as demonstrated by the child, standing in a trans-like state, however briefly, at the sight of the willow tunnel having sprouted since last observed, or the excited fervour of children discovering their hyacinth has germinated overnight!

That propensity for wonder and openness to possibility, while facilitating the free-flow of the entire being, adds credence to the conception of Truth as disclosure. The under-fives miss nothing! Possessed of general good will and immersed in the moment, young children are naturally disposed to nuances beyond the reach of most of us.

# Supporting the Spiritual

Therefore, it behoves pre-schools to provide space and time for these primal instincts. Areas of interest, such as nature, gardening, story, reflective music, dance, song and Prayer at mealtimes, or, whenever, not excluding that reflective mood generated, when children become centred, are all conducive to the spiritual.

Religious symbols and supporting literature, of which there is a great variety nowadays, all play a subliminal role. No particular Religious affiliation is a bar to the spiritual. It is part of the human condition. There is no age cohort, as disposed to the spiritual, as young children.

# Ideal Pioneers

If we are looking for a way forward, we need look no farther than our pre-school protégés. Intuitive, inquisitive, spiritual and open to possibility, young children are the ideal pioneers!

# End of Year Celebrations!

End of year celebrations complimented by the much-anticipated party was what brought life, as recorded here, to a final close. Albeit, a very exciting occasion, designed to showcase dreams come to pass and those in the making, the realisation that the adventure was over and from now on, these children would respond to different voices, brought home to me the ephemeral nature of life with all its nostalgic fallout. With the passage of time, it becomes clear that, that feeling of loss is not just a passing sentiment, but part of every human life.

If there is a moral to this story, making hay while the sun shines, might be as fitting as any!

# Conclusion

Given the imperative to relay the kinds of activities, that according to one particular parent anyway, was what pre-school education should be about, these reflections aim to do just that. Since the beginning decides the middle and the end, in the parlance of Martin Heidegger, it is no surprise then that classroom layout, structures, overall management and the inculcation of routines would set the scene for the multifaceted and progressive programme envisaged for these fledgling scholars.

Since education is understood, in the broadest of terms – from the simple puzzle, to 'stage productions' – no subject is off limits. And there is no cohort of students, as open to what is possible, than the pre-school child.

With such expectations in mind, activities from the simple to the more complex are introduced one at a time. Once children have learnt to engage with materials more independently, space is opened up for the more imaginative and interactive.

In time and buttressed by mutual bonds of understanding, trips and social occasions, introduce children to life beyond the classroom.

.med with the skills of self-management, a burgeoning
wledge base and open to 'conversation', children are well
their way to autonomy and personal well-being.